The First Rainbow
The Story of Noah

ISBN 1-84135-360-4

Copyright © 2005 Award Publications Limited

First published 2005

Published by Award Publications Limited,
27 Longford Street, London NW1 3DZ

Printed in China

The First Rainbow
The Story of Noah

by Jackie Andrews
Illustrated by Roger de Klerk

AWARD PUBLICATIONS LIMITED

Long, long ago, all the people in the world had become very wicked. It made God very sad. The only good person left was Noah.

Noah and his family loved God and served him faithfully.

One day, God told Noah he was going to wash away all the wickedness in the world with a great flood.

He wanted Noah to build a special boat,
called an ark, to keep him and his family safe,
and explained just how it should be made.

The ark had to be big enough to take Noah's family, and all the animals God wanted to save from the flood waters.

And, of course, it needed enough room to store all their food.

Noah and his sons set to work.
While they built the ark, everyone else began collecting the animals and birds.

They had to find a pair of every kind. It was
not very easy.

When the animals and birds had been collected, it was time to find enough food for them all.

At last the ark was finished and everything was ready. Noah went on board with his family, and two of every animal and bird that God wanted saved.

Seven days later, it began to rain.

It rained and rained and rained. Before long, the ark began to float on the water and was swept along by the waves.

It rained for forty days and forty nights.

Once it had stopped raining and the water had started to go down, Noah sent out a dove from the ark.

At first the dove came straight back.

The second time it brought back some olive leaves.

The third time, it did not return. Then Noah knew it was safe to leave the ark.

As everyone stepped ashore and the animals and birds were set free, Noah saw a beautiful rainbow appear in the sky. It was God's promise to Noah that he would never destroy the world again.